ARCHIPELAGOS

T0164042

ALSO BY GEOFFREY PHILP

Poetry
Exodus
Florida Bound
Hurricane Center
Xango Music
Twelve Poems and a Story for Christmas
Dubwise

Fiction
Uncle Obadiah and the Alien
Benjamin, My Son
Who's Your Daddy & Other Stories
Garvey's Ghost

Children's writing
Grandpa Sydney's Anancy Stories
Marcus and the Amazons

GEOFFREY PHILP

ARCHIPELAGOS

PEEPAL TREE

First published in Great Britain in 2023
Peepal Tree Press Ltd
17 King's Avenue
Leeds LS6 1QS
UK

© Geoffrey Philp 2023

All rights reserved
No part of this publication may be
reproduced or transmitted in any form
without permission

ISBN 13: 9781845235505

Printed in the United Kingdom
by Severn, Gloucester,
on responsibly sourced paper

MIX
Paper | Supporting
responsible forestry
FSC® C022174

Supported using public funding by
ARTS COUNCIL
ENGLAND

For Diana McCaulay

"The planet will never come alive for you unless your songs and stories give life to all the beings, seen and unseen, that inhabit a living Earth."
~ Amitav Ghosh, *The Nutmeg's Curse*

"The Earth vex."
Bob Marley, Interview, Survival Tour. 1979

CONTENTS

COLONIAL DISCOURSE

After Aimé Césaire

"At the brink of dawn", Aimé Césaire stood
on the balcony of his apartment in Martinique
and watched the sunlight spread like a rash
across the back of the city, inert as the drowned
woman floating along the Capot River, her bloated
body buoyed by waves flowing into the Caribbean
Sea, where Columbus and his crew, spurred by fever,
scoured streams, lakes, rivers for traces of gold,
and, in their delirium, ran the Santa Maria aground
in Hispaniola, where they erected a military fort
like the one in Fort-du-France occupied by French
sailors who had broken "the bonds of dependency"
by bludgeoning schoolchildren, raping their mothers,
and whipping their fathers until they folded
their arms amid squalor – never once
looking at the orange trees that blossomed
on the Carbet Peaks or at the rows of sugarcane
crushed and distilled by Le Galion that had kept
them docile for generations, dying for civilisation.

II

"At the brink of dawn", the Prefect of the Ocean
fleet, aboard the *Niña*, limping towards the coast
of Lisbon, blocked the path of a flea that had crawled
from the sleeve of his jacket over maps of the islands
of which he had taken "possession…without anyone
objecting" – not even the natives, idol-worshippers,
who, although they lived "like beasts… naked
as the day they were born", were by nature
cowards and he guaranteed his sovereign monarchs
that with fifty men they could be governed.
The journey had been a disaster. The gold he'd stolen
from the ears and hair of the Taino would not satisfy
his investors who expected more than the pineapples,
mastic gum, cotton, and the rest of the things in the hold –
eight of the Indios, who after surviving the winter, bound
in flea-infected blankets, brought the disease home.

III

For Adam Hochschild

"At the brink of dawn", Leopold II paused
to admire the blood oranges in his greenhouse
in Laeken, and felt an itch in his groin,
like when on his fiftieth birthday in London
he was accused of consorting with ten
to fifteen-year-old girls whom the mistress
of the "disorderly house" had assured him
were virgins. It was a mild irritation that in time
would go away like the dip in shipments of ivory
and rubber, whose profits he had hidden
from the Belgian Parliament in the double ledgers
he kept separate from the tally of hands
harvested from African men who, although their wives
had been held hostage, failed to meet their quota
of sap from the rubber vines. Nor did it bother him
that the crusader, Edmund Morel, had discovered
his scheme which, with Stanley's help, he'd tricked
Congolese kings into signing contracts for "vacant
land" where they had lived for generations.
No, what bothered the king was that Caroline,
his latest conquest, whom he had whisked away
from Paris when she was sixteen, had been spotted
strolling with her former lover along the bridge
he had built so he could steal away from his wife,
Henrietta, whom he hated. For after years of clawing
out his piece of Africa while conning kings, presidents,
philanthropists about his progress in spreading Christianity,
and "bringing light, faith, and trade to the dark places
of the earth", the old fox feared a pimp had outsmarted him.

IV

For Timothy Snyder

"At the brink of dawn", Adolf Hitler invigorated
by the amphetamines which his physician,
Theodore Morell – renowned for his treatment
of syphilis – had injected into his arm, summoned
his generals to report on the Schutzstaffel's expansion
of Germany's living space into Ukraine,
and the Einsatzgruppen's purge of the vermin
that had upset nature's balance in the eternal
war between the races. While his generals argued
and Himmler worried that Wehrmacht soldiers
were becoming "neurotics or savages", wading
through the brains and blood of contagion carriers,
Morell celebrated the T4 programme's success
in wiping out "useless eaters" and suggested
Zyklon B, so the troops wouldn't suffer
like one soldier, haunted by the "brown eyes"
of a six-year-old girl who, after fleeing the bunker
where her parents had been murdered, hugged
his thighs and he stabbed her with his bayonet.
The Fuhrer rubbed his hand along his leg,
where Morell had cured a worrisome
rash, and banged his fist against his desk,
signalling his approval. He could hardly wait.

V

"At the brink of dawn", the Kaiser's dream
of European colonies halted; the radio crackled
with reports of the French slaughter of freedom
fighters in Madagascar, Washington's recapture
of Guam, and parades in Paris and New York
celebrating the Allies' victory over Hitler,
who had praised Americans for gunning down
"millions of redskins" and their "progress
towards a racial empire" by "excluding certain
races from naturalization". While the Tricolor
flapped over the National Assembly, Césaire
spotted a flea, shed no doubt by the runt
that had strayed from the navy shipyard,
and at night roamed the alleys, baring its teeth
like a loup-garou, which he, as mayor,
was powerless to put down. Moving as stealthily
as one of the heroes in Senghor's stories
about Senegal, African warriors whose swords
were in the service of the broken, Césaire slipped
to the side of the balcony, holding the insect
between his index finger and thumb, and crushed
its head. A tinge of remorse shuddered
through his body as he cleaned his nails
with his handkerchief, about which he was certain
his wife, Suzanne, would gently chide him
as she ran her fingers over his nape,
as if to awaken the "power of the mahoulis".
Turning away from the dead cities sinking
under the weight of their lies, he wondered
what a new world without old masters
would resemble, when he saw Frantz loping
towards his home, his head brimming with ideas
about Négritude, and headed to the front door to greet
his former student. There was so much he had to unlearn.

OYA AWAKENED

When the pressure dropped
and Irma's path shifted toward the Keys,
lifting dust she'd carried from the Sahara,
starlings crowded into the eaves
of our house. And as we waited
in the candle-lit dark, the storm
surge reached over the seawall,
winds howled through our shutters
like the wails of Africans trapped
in the hold of slavers that followed
the same route as these hurricanes.
The trees bore the brunt of her wrath.
Only a live oak, blasted of its leaves,
stood naked in a cluster of banyans,
whose upturned roots grasp at the sun,
while the easy glide of turkey buzzards
over choked canals revealed the sudden
beauty of clearings across the skyline.

ARCHIPELAGOS
After Derek Walcott

At the end of this sentence, a flood will rise
and swallow low-lying islands of the Caribbean,
like when Hurricane Maria whipped the Atlantic
into a ring of thunderstorms that advanced
in the way Auerbach described her vision of terror:
"Wooden huts torn away from their foundations
were carried away, women and children were tied
to the ceiling beams, but no one could see a tangle
of arms waving from the roof, like branches
blowing in the wind, waving desperately toward
heaven toward the river banks for help";
and a man, chest-deep in the surge that snatched
his family from his arms in seas swelling
before him, like Columbus and his crew
imagined Leviathan, "whose mere sight
is overpowering", who "looked down on all
that is haughty." But wasn't it pride, greed —
those sins we've forgotten, for they remind us
of what we could have become instead of what
we've settled for — that extended our reach,
like the virus with its crown of spikes,
around the waist of the world to the polar
ice caps, melting into the ocean that's rising
one inch every three years in Miami,
where leatherbacks lumber out of the water
to lay their eggs as carefully as I swaddle
my grandniece in a blanket, scenes my daughter
remembers in the same breath with the bumper
sticker on the first car I owned, "Save the Whales",
the protests where we marched before she could walk,
the war she inherited along with my grandmother's
hair — that simple country girl from St. James,
home to Sam Sharpe and the Maroons who fought

redcoats, whose bayonets were stained with the blood
of Africans kidnapped from huts under the growl
of the harmattan's sweep over the Sahara
to the rim of the Cape Verde Islands, garlanded
by trade winds that complete the circle and begin
a new alphabet of catastrophe – hurricanes that stagger
like a betrayed lover barrelling through the islands
until its rage is spent on the sands of our beaches
littered with masks and plastic bottles.

A SURVIVAL GUIDE

For Tathiana Patino

When you reach the place
where every strategy you've devised
to keep disaster away from your door
is crushed like the lifeboat you were sure
would keep you safe from the water
that's rising above your ankles, waist,
neck, and you think, Why not simply fall
into the wreckage tickling the tips
of your toes as you tread toward the skylight?

Then, with bruised fingers, you must feel
along the cracks of what's left of the roof
to find an opening, and bind the splintered
rafters floating near your shoulder with rope,
twine, lianas, anything the flood throws up
from the swamp you've combed since the island
of mangroves near the coast were saplings
in the brine of the bayou, their leaves as bright
as the crystals in your submerged Go Bag,
to take you where there's a fire, a respite
from dread, so when the next hurricane howls
over the top of the levees — and it will — you'll be ready
to endure the brokenness of the world's beauty.

AFTER THE HURRICANE

For Lizabeth Paravisini-Gebert

"Just breathe," I said to my wife as she rubbed
her eyes and looked down the throat of the estuary,
choked with red algae, *Karenia brevis*, the beauty
of its bloom dulled by our knowledge of its toxins,
fed by pollution from as far away as the Mississippi
and as near as Indian River, water laden with poisons
that seep into seagrass, into the lungs of manatees,
flesh of sharks, carapaces of crabs – victims of our addiction,
our quest for "gold, sugar, rum", the mantra repeated
by a griot, who scrawled crowns of the dispossessed
on walls of the city that slept on the banks of the Hudson,
his grief for black bodies, disposable as sea
turtles, washed up on the sand, gasping for air –
the debris of empires that crowd our shores.

The first insult was the bodies
of warriors huddled in the hold
of slavers like the *Zong*,
and the captain, low on fresh water,
led elders to the stern and prodded
them with swords until they plunged
feet first into the froth that held
their arms afloat for a moment
and then swallowed them into the blue,
their bones strewn over the Atlantic,
which every June, when the harmattan
gathers clouds over the seabed, lashes
coconut fronds until skies turn as dark
as Eshu's eyes scanning barrier islands,
pelts tourists, helpless as starfish
stranded on dunes, with hail – the lies
of fathers visited upon their children:
her anger spilling over the sea wall
down Las Olas, where sharks and small
fish navigate the shuttered storefronts.

A GATHERING OF THE ORISHAS

Fallen, salt-burned leaves
mango blossoms in the yard
Osain's teardrops.

Water at my door –
the wrath of Oya.

A bloom of red tide
Six hundred tons of dead fish
in Xango's footsteps.

Along the shore's edge
Indian River sparkles
with alms to Oshun.

Biscayne's coral reef
white as Yemaya's bracelets –
bleached of her mercy

In the dry season
Ogun's breath sends sparks flying
to the Everglades

On morning TV
hosts promise bright days ahead
to Eshu's cackles

STILL, I RISE
After Maya Angelou

Still, I rise above the hot zones
that spread across America, like the heatwave
in the eighties when thirty-two deaths a day
from an act of God was a national tragedy.

Still, I rise over the roofs of nursing homes
where grandparents died alone; factories
of death where meat cutters, shoulder-to-shoulder,
fell on the floor of assembly lines; a hospital
where a man gasps for air, and a woman snores
comfortably in her bed; a boy plays with a toy
gun to the drone of hacks on television arguing
about the pros and cons of a lie and unmasked
resisters cough in the faces of passersby.

Still, I rise every morning before the sun
has graced the leaves of live oaks with diamonds,
to jog in a park where my father, who hasn't flown
a kite in over fifty years, has built with yarn, bamboo,
glue, and tissue paper a bajie as strong as his desire
to savour the tartness of tangerines before breakfast;
the aroma of mint from a garden he started a year
ago, the turpentine of Julie mangoes from a tree
he planted at the birth of his first grand who huddles
around his thin frame and waits for the moment
when the cord will come alive in his hands,
and the kite will soar above pines shading
families who celebrate the miracles of green
near a lake where anhingas, perched on dead logs,
stretch their wings to dry their feathers –
ready to brave another flight into the sun.

THE TRIGGER

It isn't the hacking cough, like the ones
that terrified me when my father would reach
for his pack of Benson & Hedges, instead of a belt,
before his long walk down the driveway
where he would exhale smoke and gaze
at rain clouds hovering over Long Mountain,
or the shortness of breath, like my mother's
gasp, two months after she ended up in the ICU
of Memorial Hospital when she confessed
that she'd neglected to remove a mole
that'd been bothering her, or even the fever,
like when my daughter, who was barely five,
saw spiders crawling up the foot of her bed,
and I, a young father, could only cradle her
in my arms. No, what scares me –
although I'd stared three times into the chamber
of a revolver during Jamaica's undeclared civil
war – was the time when our family went to Gun
Boat Beach and I slipped off a rock, my arms flailing
before I shuffled back to the sandbar with the fear
that never left me, of disappearing under the waves.

HAIKUS FOR THE END OF THE WORLD

Crisp morning glories
line the pathway on my walk
beside withered trees

Ghost buses rumble
past an empty bus shelter
while finches build nests.

Outside our Publix
homeless men who searched for butts
fidget on a bench

The Goodwill's doors closed,
the homeless man who reads books
finds newfound treasures

A murder of crows
taunts a schizophrenic girl
by stealing her bread

In the parking lot
pouis burn a bright yellow –
sentinels of hope

VIRTUAL THANKSGIVING

Inside a local supermarket, open for last-
minute shoppers – nurses, cashiers, waiters,
front line workers who can't afford a day off –
I lost track of time as I hurried through aisles
laden with sweet potato pies and candied yams,
in search of painkillers to relieve my migraines
that have flared since the virus crept into our lives,
and glimpsed a cornucopia, like the one I'd seen
with my mother on our first Thanksgiving
when I confessed I couldn't enjoy a holiday
that celebrated colonisers, who repaid
Wampanoag hospitality by beheading
the Massasoit's son, or how undercover
agents had spurred sufferers, who had borne
the insults of empire, to unleash anarchy
on our streets, murder on our beaches.

As she stared at the horn filled with plums,
pears and pomegranates spilling over the rim,
tears rolled down my mother's cheeks
when she remembered the empty shelves
she'd left the year before when she promised
to send for my sister and me.

Yet she listened patiently and said, "I hope
you won't become a man who measures his life
by hard times, by sorrows that hide in our closets,
lingering in the corners of our rooms, for grief
can twist you into someone you barely recognise
in the mirror before you plunge into traffic
and the busyness of paperwork and bills.
I am grateful that my mother left the bustle
of Montego Bay to live in Westmoreland
with my father, who sold his last cow

so I could attend teachers' college
in Kingston and that today – even if it's only
the three of us – we can share a meal."

While I waited in the checkout lane
with other masked customers, my phone
buzzed with a text from my wife – I was late
for the family meeting. My headache could wait.
I left the bottle on the counter and headed home
to raise my glass with my sister in Orlando,
my children in Georgia and Miami, cousins
in Colombia, each on a private screen.
For though we'd celebrate a virtual Thanksgiving
in this year when so many chairs
are missing at our tables, it is sufficient grace.

ANTHROPOCENE SUITE

For Amitav Ghosh

Peel the pale, brown flesh
hold the cracked shell to your ear:
screams of the Banda.

Escaping Earth's hold,
unmanned rockets race to claim
living space on Mars.

My compass shivers
while Antarctica loses ice
shifting the North Pole.

In Siberia,
a crater's jaw swallows hills –
a black hole to hell.

From blue to yellow
the mighty Mississippi
changes her make-up.

On Miami Beach
Humvees drown in parking lots
under King Tide's reign.

Along Hellshire's coast
the Carib Sea has reclaimed
Terra nullius.

Like incense, prayers rise
from our once sacred rivers,
from Oshun's children.

A TERRIBLE BEAUTY

When the *MV Express Pearl*, carrying twenty-five
tons of nitric acid and seventy-eight tons of plastic
pellets, lurched into the port of Colombo, sailors

released carbon dioxide into the hold to put out a fire
that had been smoldering for two weeks. But it was too late.
The ship keeled from an explosion of the acid and hurled

plastic pellets into the air, which descended on the yellow
sands of Sri Lanka in a flutter of unmelting snow that glittered
at sunrise, like the stone Devair Alves Ferreira bought

from two junkyard scavengers. Intrigued by the blue
light, Devair shaved granules from the stone and shared
the poison of cesium 137 with his family and friends

in Goiânia until his wife's hair fell out in clumps
on the bathroom floor. And while the Brazilian police
brought the men responsible to justice for the theft

of a radioactive canister from an abandoned lab,
competing adjusters are now shifting blame to India and Qatar,
which denied entry to their harbours because they didn't want

the problem in their backyard. But tell that to the soldier
scraping debris from the backs of crabs, who fears
the pellets will raise the temperature of the sand in nesting

grounds of turtles, when a generation of single-sex
hatchlings will crawl into the sea. Or tell that
to fishermen who can no longer feed their families
as the ship sinks and the ocean burns.

SONGS OF THE ARCHIPELAGOS

For Small Island, Big Song

They come from places you could easily forget,
somewhere between the Pacific and Indian
Oceans: islands where statues gaze at the horizon,
like when the ancestors in deep time first
launched their canoes, not knowing if or when
they'd return to the caress of their loved ones,
risked the currents and disappeared into the mist.
Yet they sing, despite the threats of cyclones,
love songs to their children, barely out of diapers
but old enough to recognise what the stutter
in their mothers' voices means – maybe the waters
creeping up the stilts of their home, year after year,
is a sign that the ways of the elders will be lost
when heads of yam, stems of taro are drowned in salt.

THE FOREST WOMAN

For Diana Beresford-Kroeger

Maybe it was the streak of wildness in her veins
why they called her an outlier, for she believed

in the stories from a long line of medicine women
who shared cures for commons ailments – Druids

who taught that the Earth was connected to heaven –
poultices from wildflowers, like shamrocks, contained

flavonoids which increased blood flow, and St John's
Wort could help to raise a man from off his bed.

But when she heard the roar of bikes from the local
Hell's Angels, collecting saplings for their property

from the forest she had created in her backyard,
she knew it was a sign, as clear as the chemical

messages mycelia send to the roots of trees,
that the change she'd feared had already started.

AMERICAN WELCOME

I'll never forget the first time
when, as a recent arrival to America,
I'd taken a fellowship for a month-long
residency in Seaside, Florida (where no two
houses on the same street are allowed
to have the same picket fence), and eager
to escape the white noise of the Lyceum,
modelled after Jefferson's academic village,
where I'd been dubbed "the equal opportunity
candidate", I wandered outside the gates
on my morning jog, as if I was still
that privileged schoolboy who could go
anywhere he wanted, when a pickup
truck with six or so rednecks, swilling
beer on a flatbed – they might as well have been
on a hunt and wearing white robes –
pulled over to the other side of the road.
A bottle whizzed by while I was tying
my shoe laces and they screamed, "Niggerrrrrrrrrrr!"
I looked behind me to find the target
of their anger, for Garvey had taught me
long ago never to answer to that name,
and then jumped out of the way
before another bottle exploded near my feet.
I continued my journey toward
the outskirts of the town, but now always
looking over my shoulder, always
running, always out of breath.

PHILOSOPHY 101

I'd avoided the class until my senior year in college
when my advisor warned me that I wouldn't graduate
until I took a course on western philosophy,
in which, as I feared, instead of reading the discussions
between Camus, the pied-noir writer who argued
for the State's use of force, and Sartre, who enlisted
Fanon to untangle Hegel's Master-Slave dialectic,
we read Kant's theses about the nature of evil and good.

Two weeks later, my suspicions about the course
were confirmed when the TA, fresh out of graduate
school, decided to assign a thought experiment.
It was a simple exercise, he explained,
in which we'd follow – without relying on emotions,
for they always led to invalid conclusions – the logic
of our premises. "Suppose you had to choose
between saving an irreplaceable painting, let's say
a Rembrandt – who bathes his subjects in light
while pushing darkness to the edge of the frame –
or the life of an old woman, who'd lived long enough
to see her grandchildren, so she didn't have much
to look forward to, what would be your choice?
The paper's due next week."

Trudging back to my dorm, I doubted
if the answer would have been so simple
if his grandmother had been forced
into the bowels of the *Zong* or, on another
continent, been herded into showers
in Buchenwald, where scholars, who'd studied
Nietzsche found a haven in the officer's
quarters while ash from the chimneys
clouded windows of their favourite theatres.

I would've dropped the course, but the deadline
had already passed, so I plopped on my bed
and studied the ceiling tiles when D., my roommate,
sprouting dreadlocks, saw me scratching my head.
"What are you struggling with?" he asked. I showed
him the assignment, and he said. "These guys don't get it.
Rastafari knows everything begins with I am, therefore,
I wonder. Don't follow dem fuckry, me bredrin,
not one raas." So I took a gamble and skipped
writing the paper. No wonder I failed that class.

ROADMAP TO GENOCIDE
For Gregory H. Stanton

First, you'll need a leader who carries a burden
from which he can find no relief from the lies
he invents, so he has to search for someone, anyone
to blame for his misery, for the torments of his warriors
who aren't afraid to crack a few skulls of niggers,
kikes, gypsies – you name the brutes. Don't worry.
They're more like cockroaches, rats, lice, parasites,
that leech the blood of children; vermin that transmit
diseases like typhus, AIDS, Ebola, monkeypox
and others, which your scientists haven't yet
identified, but for which the cure is always quarantine
in camps as far away as Krome from Miami.

But be careful. Begin by organising the police,
army, militia – what have you – and if you're lucky,
you may recruit half-breeds who are willing to fatten
themselves by enforcing laws that keep them weak –
statutes you've devised to keep your women safe
from the caravans of criminals crossing the border
with one intent – to finger your daughter's hair,
to grope her thighs with their greasy hands
and germs under their fingernails.

The rest of the journey should be easy – whether
you want slaves or to capture things they had no right
in the first place to possess. Choose your methods
judiciously. No one will notice a murder, here or there,
until trials are underway, and if you've done
the groundwork, only a few protesters will remain,
for the other resisters have disappeared. Don't leave
evidence lying around, so when you reach your final
destination, you'll see signs like *"Arbeit macht frei"*.

TARGET PRACTICE

After Jericho Brown

I ride around this city, feeling as if I'm always a target,
like the ones at a gun range where cops used mug shots
of African-American men to improve the shots
of their snipers – photos of black men who weren't dead
but whose images would help to kill the soon-to-be-dead
on the way back from the library, a party, or even a drag race.
For although I don't trust the spokesperson who said that race
had nothing to do with the department's choice of pictures,
I believe him when he said they would be adding pictures
from the database of suspects that they've arrested,
so when I'm pulled over, I know I'm going to be arrested.
I ride around this city, feeling as if I'm always a target.

PRECAUTIONARY MEASURES

My son used to think that his mother
was being dramatic when before every trip
across the state, she would make a sign
of the cross on his forehead and hug him
as if she would never see him again.
But what he didn't know was that every
time he borrowed my car to run an errand,
or while he was out doing what teenagers
love to do, play video games, maybe get
lucky, I was whispering a prayer –
even though I haven't been to church
since my mother died – to keep Babylon
away from my boy, so he wouldn't be pulled
over for "Failure to signal before turning
into a parking lot", or that old chestnut,
"Suspicious activity in the neighbourhood."
For when you live one step away
from the catch-as-catch-can genocide
that hides in the swirling lights of police
cars, you doubt whether prayer can protect
loved ones from the evil of men doing their job.

BAD FRIDAY

For Deborah A. Thomas and John L. Jackson

Years after the beasts of Babylon
swooped down on Pinnacle and scattered
Rastafari, whose wisdom became flesh
for I to unlearn the folly of Rose Hall,
the bald heads grabbed I in Coral Gardens
on a bright Good Friday morning and scream,
"Rasta bwai, you a go dead today."

It never matter that I come from a good
family or that I mother raise I with good
manners – "Howdy and tenky bruk no square" –
the Babylon only need to see I beard –
evidence I would never bow to the image
of the massa – for them to beat I naked
like Jehsus Christus before the Roman
soldiers heng him like a tief on a tree.

And all I could hear was the whoosh
of batons raining on I crown
until the light leave I head.
But even in darkness, I sight up
the glory of His Majesty and stay
as still as a spider waiting for I deliverance.
For in the hour of I tribulation, when it feel
as if the Father turn Him back, like just before
a hurricane when man-o-war come home
to roost, I overstand that even in the depths
of hell, I&I would rise into full-fullness
on the wings of mourning doves over Mount Salem.

HOW TO SPOT A SURVIVOR

I don't know what you did, but whatever
you did, it was wrong. So wrong that the soldiers
(or anyone carrying a knife, gun, machete,
or lacking a weapon, improvised with their hands)
murdered your family on a day so beautiful,
the chamber of commerce could've used a photo
to entice tourists to visit your country –
that is before the State Department's travel
ban inched across the television – your companion
that silences the questions that keep returning:
Did you do too much or too little?
And the drugs you use to fall asleep
make matters worse. For when you dream,
hands drag you back into the earth,
and you keep hoping it's an elaborate
prank, and that on your next birthday
or the next one after that, when you open
the door to your too-small apartment –
which could've never held gatherings
of your rambunctious family – they'll pop
up from behind the sofa and yell, "Surprise!";
and your mother, whom your aunt says
you resemble, though you can't see
the similarity even after you've studied
her photographs from every angle,
will one day appear behind you
when you're staring in the mirror
to nod approvingly at the reflection;
or even your father, whom you despised
for the beatings you would now gladly
endure when he came home drunk
and grabbed anything he could lay his hands
on: a shoe, an extension cord, a tamarind switch
as if placed in his way by an avenging angel

to beat the feistiness out of you; or your brother,
who was always broke, you wish was beside you.
Still broke, but not dead. And how could he be dead
when he was the only one who could explain
why you feel as if you are in a deleted chapter of *Left
Behind* because you and the murderers are still alive?

A SEARCH FOR ANCESTORS

Down narrow corridors of the Muskowekwan
School for Indigenous Children, we enter
the nightmare of our guide, Harry Desjarlais,
who'd been kidnapped and herded into dorms
with beds as long as caskets in a potter's field.

The walls flake with tongues of paint
that speak the language in which he cried,
that his teachers scrubbed from his mouth,
so he could become a civilised Christian,
and not grow up a pagan like his parents.

Inside a shower, Harry pauses
where he'd found a classmate's body –
the one who always made fun of nuns
with their dull habits and veils, white
as the cloth on God's table where he prayed
ten times a day to be released from the priests'
torture and discovered Heaven's gates
were closed to the people of his nation.

As we descend, we're greeted by screams
of children playing hide-and-seek
atop unmarked graves of ancestors –
some younger than Harry's granddaughter –
before they walked into the bonfire
from which we light bundles of sage
and smudge our bodies so as not to disturb
the spirits who've earned their rest.

In the courtyard, while boxcars rattle
towards unknown destinations, we lug
ground-penetrating radar – whose reflections
we weave into a quilt of images that resemble

a weatherman's screen pockmarked with red
tornado cells, scouring the open fields,
ready to sweep the candles and cascade of teddy
bears crouched on the steps of the school
into bison-crowded prairies on hallowed ground.

THE ARCHANGEL'S TRUMPET

If you followed the frescoes on the ceiling
of the Sistine Chapel, you'd believe
that there are no black angels in heaven.
And, maybe, they are right. Our seraphs
and cherubs would rather help Yemaya
protect her children from the wolves
in this world than spend eternity
pondering the mysteries of the Madonna's
Assumption. And although being in the form
of God who weeps for the blood shed
on our sidewalks and in our bedrooms,
they emptied themselves when they took on
the likeness of men and women in the land of Dis –
dishonour, disrespect, disregard, desgraciada –
where black skin is despised like an incurable disease –
the darker the hue, the greater the sin,
and the only cure is a bullet or a noose.
But in those moments when we put aside
our mortal concerns – paying doctors' bills
or worrying if our spouses and children
will make it home for dinner –
when we have grown tired of hiding
grimaces behind selfies and mug shots,
we unfurl wings that cover backs
scarred by the spite of downpressers,
wounds from those whom we love so dearly,
and re-join the hymns that we knew before
our feet landed on the sand, on the auction
block, before we had forgotten how to fly
and lift our voices to a sky that greets
the chorus, the way flamehearts signal
the start of summer with crimson petals,
with the harmony of bees on a pollen path,
we recognise the opening bars: "Blow your trumpet,

Gabriel, Blow your trumpet louder; I want
dat trumpet to blow me home to my new Jerusalem."

AMERICA 2020

America, you've lost your way.
You've believed in your innocence
for so long you've betrayed your promises
on parchment, robbed fatherless children
of their birthright, trapped children in cages,
and while the oceans churn towards a slow boil,
and a virus holds us hostage in our homes,
you've allowed gangsters to prey on families
seeking asylum from thugs
in Honduras, El Salvador, and Guatemala.
And you'd rather die than give up your privilege
to hunt black men you think have become too uppity.
Now for the millions lost in the Maafa,
massacres in East St. Louis, Tulsa, Rosewood,
the destruction of Overtown, and the poisoning
of Flint, we are marking stones where our martyrs
have fallen, taking note of your crimes that fester
like scraps of flesh – desperate offerings
to the saints for justice – littering the steps
of the courthouse in Miami, where a wake
of turkey buzzards returns to their roosts atop
skyscrapers every winter, their wings darkening the skies

CREOLE WARRIOR
For Colette Pinchon Battle

Born on the Bayou in the eye of the storm,
Co-co had learned when to be calm or afraid
on her family's land where people of colour

had bought their freedom long before America
knew her name, before the levees, which the Army
Corps built, had failed and New Orleans,

celebrated for carnivals of flesh and debauchery,
became a black spot on a map the sea reclaimed.
When Katrina's floodwaters defiled the places

she had called holy – the aged oaks on the high
ground near the house her grandfather built –
and tainted with muck after a thirty-foot tidal surge

swept away bodies, like refuse from slavers;
and the water table never recovered from salt
intrusion, Co-co, like her mother, joined

the fight for her people to be heard, over the slow
grinding jaws of the swamp, to dismantle
codes that govern those "unworthy of life" – the laws FEMA

enforced when the director said, "We are seeing
people we never knew existed", and drew a line
as precise as the *nec plus ultra* that separated

the habitable temperate zones centered in Jerusalem
from the uninhabitable torrid zones west of the Pillars
of Hercules, places outside God's grace, justly punishable,

as Odysseus and his upstart crew had been for breaching
the inviolable, damned, even if all the oil rigs shut
down their wells – their flares like beacons in the Gulf.

A RECKONING

It could have been on a day like this
when Pero Jones, an enslaved African,
who had worked well for Edward Pinney's

family in Bristol, drowned his grief in rum
when they took him back to their plantation
in Nevis, on a visit from England,

to where he returned and died in his master's
house in the country. And for over a hundred years,
the descendants of Pero Jones grew tired

of the pain – like the kind George Floyd's
brother confessed in his testimony before Congress –
of the daily insult when they faced Edward Colston's

statue ("Erected by the citizens of Bristol
as a memorial to one of the most virtuous and wise
sons of the city") that sneered when they crossed

the footbridge named after their ancestor,
until Bristolians eventually grabbed their hammers
and enough rope to support the weight of a man,

and tore down the statue and dumped it in Bristol Harbour
where centuries before, Colston's ships, after selling
their payload of sugar – served in the finest teahouses

in the Empire – returned to Elmina Castle
to retrieve his property, branded with the seal
of the Royal African Company on their chests,

and then slipped past the sharks, following
for cargo dumped unfit for sale into the ocean,
their sails billowed by winds, which later

became the hurricanes that now threaten
windmills, Great Houses, statues of conquistadors
and criminals in the archipelago of the dispossessed.

HISTORY LESSON

Inside my father's darkened study,
lined with thumb-worn history books,
and portraits of his heroes, warrior saints,
like Ignatius Loyola, whom he adored
from when he was about the same age
as my son, to whom he hands a globe
to show the old borders before the world
went to hell. My father's index finger
traces along the meridians with the ease
that another of his heroes, Pope Julius,
made a line that ran through the Cape
Verde Islands to the Nuremberg Laws
that separated the damned from the saved.
And despite my unease with this lesson —
quieted by his glance that paralyses
my hands — I cannot tear my son away
from his arms, for he is my father,
and I am a good son who must obey.

ANTHEM FOR THE WOKE

Where are the protestors from the summer of plague
who saw Black lives threatened, and marched to free
us from fascists and were greeted by an army of fear-
mongers united in their cause to make sure change
would never happen, and began a campaign of lies
among the afflicted to sate the elites' lust for power,

that revealed their resistance to Black power –
the rising numbers in the cities they see as a plague,
so every cable series or news story is filled with lies
about Black crime – dire warnings that if we're ever free,
no one will be free, for we will have changed
America for the worse, and everyone will live in fear.

It's what Public Enemy was rapping about in *Fear
of a Black Planet,* especially in "Fight the Power",
so we'd start the process of believing in the change
that must happen at the top, or else we'll be plagued
by doubters who will delay our quest for freedom
from their lies. For they lie. They lie. They lie.

But what if we stopped believing their lies,
the denials and gaslighting that keep them in fear
of shadows they've invented – that won't set them free
until they've given up their need for control, for power,
at the cost of the planet's life – before we're plagued
by circumstances we won't be able to change

once the irreversible effects of climate change –
which oil company CEOs have labelled as a lie –
melts ice caps and releases viruses to plague
future generations, who will live in perpetual fear
of the next hurricane, heatwaves that disrupt power
grids, melt electric cables, will fresh air still be free?

The ancestors' promise lives in the struggle to be free.
Ancestors like Marcus and Malcolm, who tried to change
our minds about the hold of the empire's power
over our people who have been educated with lies
about our past while others, paralysed with fear,
stare into the future as if it were a plague.

Rise, once again, and free yourselves from the lies
that keep us cowering in the dark. Rise, change your fear
from a plague of doubt into a power that liberates.

THE ADMIRAL

Freed by an obeah woman, who wanted
"a likkle company every Friday evening",
the Admiral, when everyone else was asleep,
would crawl down his pedestal to answer
the summons to her bed, where he'd stay
until midnight and then ascend to his rightful
position, the title he once bore, Viceroy of the Indies.

But it has been three years since his liberator
died, yet her curse remains. Now the Admiral
heads straight to the cemetery to pay respects
to his mistress, climbs to her shack at the top
of Liberty Hill to claim part of the inheritance
she'd hidden under her floor, and where he keeps
sun-bleached clothes he'd stolen from the poor
on Windsor Road – like a common thief –
so he could roam anonymous among these
New World Africans, until the rumheads
renamed him "The Cuban" because of his accent.

The Admiral hated that name. He preferred
the name his mother, Susanna, had given him,
Cristoffa Corombo, whispered in the soft syllables
of her Ligurian tongue. But at least it was better
than what one dreadlocked African, whom the Admiral
would have sworn had figured out his identity,
called him: "Christopher-Come-Buck-Us."

Grabbing his clothes, the Admiral walked past women
selling cheap goods from Cathay – as if the Silk Road
had reached Xaymaca – to his favourite bar near the Negro
River, which reminded him of the tavern that Domenico,
his father, had owned in Savona, where he'd learned
the secrets of ocean winds and stories about fabled

Cipangu. But everywhere had been discovered,
and when the Admiral entered the bar, he ordered
his usual shot of rum from Rosie, a beautiful African
woman, whom he'd have loved to draw but was afraid
she'd be offended. The last thing the Admiral needed
was angry Africans poking into his business.

Gripping the shot glass between his thumb and index
finger with the same firmness as he'd held pens
when he signed letters demanding justice from the Spanish
court – pleadings that were never resolved –
the Admiral watched the news on the television –
a miracle if he ever saw one – about the toppling
of Edward Colston's statue. And though their nations
had always been at war, they were allies in the same
cause, so the Admiral retreated to the back of the bar
where he settled among the shadows and sipped
his drink until a group of Africans, led by the dreadlocked
one, sat in front of the television, blocking his view.

Though furious at the effrontery, the Admiral held
his anger and shifted his chair. His mistress
had tutored him in the ways of the island,
but he'd never grown accustomed to the speech
of these Africans. He moved his chair to eavesdrop
on the conversation that had captured his attention.

"Tear him raas off de rock," said the dreadlocked
African, who had escaped the enchantment of empire
by studying his reflection. As the images burned
on the screen, the Admiral gulped down the rest
of his drink and signalled to Rosie for another shot
when he saw the beheading of his statue in Boston,
the drowning of another in Richmond and realised
that the African's plan would mean his second death.

"Grind de marble to dus' and dash it inna de sea,"
one of the other Africans added. The Admiral wanted
to object. "But I was a messenger of Christ,
and the Word of God has now spread to the four
corners of the world – a sign that the Second
Coming is that hand!" But he also remembered
what had happened in Española to the nine
year-old girls he'd procured for his Castellanos,
but knew, if he still possessed the power he once
wielded, he'd have cut out their tongues,
as his brother, Bartolomeo, had done
to a woman who had claimed that their family
had descended from common stock; or sliced
off their ears, as his men had done to the Indios,
"to test the sharpness of their blades."

But when the Africans raised their glasses
in a toast, "To Christopher Come-Be-Louse.
Deadman walking", the Admiral felt a tremor
had shaken the foundation of the island.
The Admiral wanted to run away, but where?
He was duty-bound to answer the call of overseeing
the town, so he waited for the last African to leave
before he paid his debt for the night with Rosie,
who asked, "Same time next week, Cuban?"

The Admiral grunted goodbye, and as he staggered
up Main Street, he wondered when he'd hear
the sound of Africans marching along the Roaring
River, sunlight glinting off their machetes, the tools
of their ancestors, chanting the words of their liberator,
"We must emancipate ourselves from mental slavery."

ACKNOWLEDGMENTS

Grateful acknowledgment is made to the following publications in which these poems or earlier versions first appeared (sometimes with different titles):

Poets Reading the News: "Oya Awakened," "After the Hurricane."
WritersMosaic: "Archipelagos."
Anthropocene, "A Gathering of the Orishas."
Topical Poetry: "Still, I Rise."
Indolent Books: "Haikus for the End of the World."
The New Verse News: "A Terrible Beauty."
Topical Poetry, "Songs of the Archipelagos"
The Punch Magazine: "Roadmap to Genocide," "A Reckoning" and "History Lessons."
Canopic Jar 35: "How to Spot a Survivor," "Philosophy 101."
Writers Resist: "Target Practice."
South Florida Poetry Journal: "America 2020"
Visible Magazine "A Search for Ancestors"
Interviewing the Caribbean, "Creole Warrior"
Pree. Caribbean. Writing: "The Admiral"

LIVICATION

Give thanks to Dennis Scott, Anthony McNeill, Mervyn Morris, Kamau Brathwaite, Olive Senior, Lorna Goodison, Pam Mordecai and Derek Walcott, whose poems made it possible for me to imagine my life as a writer. Thank you, Monique Roffey, Colin Grant, and WritersMosaic, for commissioning "Archipelagos," which helped me bring together many of the themes in this book and gave me a much-needed confidence boost during the lockdown. Thank you, Patricia Saunders, David Scott, and Small Axe, for commissioning "The Archangel's Trumpet." Thanks to Kei Miller, who graciously allowed me to sit in on his creative writing workshop at the 37th Annual Meeting of the West Indian Literature Conference, Global Caribbean Studies: Scapes, at the University of Miami, where I learned so much. I am grateful to Deborah Biggs, Jonathan Plutzik, and the Betsy Hotel, whose support has been invaluable for completing this manuscript. Thank you, Sudeep Sen, for your insightful comments about "Colonial Discourse" and Don Krieger and Indran Amirthanayagam for bringing my work to a broader audience. My gratitude to Jeremy Poynting, Kwame Dawes, Hannah Bannister, and Peepal Tree Press for their continued support of my work and the work of Caribbean, Black British, and Asian writers. Thank you to my family for believing in me and surrounding me with so much love. And speaking of love, thank you, Nadia, for everything.

NOTES ON THE POEMS

The quotes used in "Colonial Discourse" were from the following sources:

p. 9. "At the brink of dawn," *Notebook of a Return to my Native Land* by Aime Cesaire (trans. Mireille Rosello and Annie Pritchard) Bloodaxe Books.

p. 9. "the bonds of dependency" *Discourse on Colonialism* by Aime Cesaire (trans. Joan Pinkham) Monthly Review Press.

p. 10. "possession…without anyone objecting" – not even the natives, who although they lived "like beasts…naked as the day they were born" *The Journal of Christopher Columbus by Christopher Columbus, et al.*, Bonanza Books, 1989.

p. 11. "disorderly house" *King Leopold's Ghost: A Study of Greed, Terror, and Heroism in Colonial Africa* by Adam Hochschild, Papermac, 2000.

p. 11. "vacant land" *King Leopold's Ghost: A Study of Greed, Terror, and Heroism in Colonial Africa* by Adam Hochschild, Papermac, 2000.

p. 11. "bringing light, faith and trade to the 'dark places' of the earth," The Dead Do Not Die: *Exterminate All the Brutes* by Sven Lindqvist, The New Press, 1992.

p. 12. "neurotics or savages" *Hitler's Holocaust* by Guido Knopp, Sutton Publishing, 2004.

p. 12. "useless eaters" "Nazi Persecution of the Disabled: Murder of the 'Unfit.'" *United States Holocaust Memorial Museum*, www.ushmm.org/information/exhibitions/online-exhibitions/special-focus/nazi-persecution-of-the-disabled.

p. 12. "brown eyes" "The Nazis Pursuit for a 'Humane' Method of Killing'" Understanding Willing Participants Milgram's Obedience Experiments and the Holocaust by Nestar Russell, *Palgrave Macmillan*, 2019.

p. 13. "millions of redskins," "progress towards a racial empire" by "excluding certain races from naturalization." "How American Racism Influenced Hitler." *The New Yorker* by Alex Ross www.newyorker.com/magazine/2018/04/30/how-american-racism-influenced-hitler.

"power of the mahoulis" (Nov 01, 1999) Topics: Imperialism. "A Poetics of Anticolonialism." *Monthly Review* by Robin D.G. Kelley, 13 Oct. 2015, monthlyreview.org/1999/11/01/a-poetics-of-anticolonialism/.

p. 15. "wooden huts torn away from their foundations were carried away, women and children were tied to the ceiling beams, but no one could see a tangle of arms waving from the roof, like branches blowing in the wind, waving desperately toward heaven toward the river banks for help." "Yizkor, 1943" by Rachel Auerbach.

p. 15. "whose mere sight is overpowering," "looked down on all that is haughty." Job 41:9 and 34, *New International Version*.

p. 37. Pinnacle, the first Rastafari community in Jamaica was founded in 1940 by Rastafari elder Leonard Howell. Based on Marcus Garvey's ideas of Black pride and self-reliance, the free village flourished until 1954, when the colonial authorities demolished it.

p. 42. "Blow your trumpet, Gabriel, /Blow your trumpet louder; I want dat trumpet to blow me home to my new Jerusalem." in "The Archangel's Trumpet" was from the following source: https://www.negrospirituals.com/songs/blow_you_trumpet_gabriel.htm

p. 52. The quote used to end "The Admiral" was from the following source: "We must emancipate ourselves from mental slavery" *The Philosophy and Opinions of Marcus Garvey* by Marcus Garvey, Majority Press.

Epigraphs: "The Earth vex," Interview with Bob Marley, https://youtu.be/ld_UuPVPWNQ

ABOUT THE AUTHOR

Geoffrey Philp is a Jamaican author of poetry, short stories, novels and children's books. He teaches creative writing at Miami Dade College and has a Master of Arts in English from the University of Miami. Peepal Tree has published seven of his books. A huge supporter of Caribbean books and writers, he posts interviews, fiction, poetry, podcasts, and literary events from the Caribbean and South Florida on his blog.

Born in Kingston, Jamaica, Geoffrey Philp attended Mona Primary and Jamaica College, where he studied literature under the tutelage of Dennis Scott. After leaving Jamaica in 1979, he went to Miami Dade College and after graduating, he studied Caribbean, African and African-American literature with Dr. O.R. Dathorne and creative writing with Lester Goran, Evelyn Wilde Mayerson, and Isaac Bashevis Singer. As a James Michener Fellow at the University of Miami, he studied poetry with Kamau Brathwaite and fiction with George Lamming.

In 1990, he published his first book of poems, *Exodus and Other Poems*; five other poetry collections have followed: *Florida Bound* (1995), *hurricane center* (1998), *xango music* (2001), and *Twelve Poems and A Story for Christmas* (2005) and *Dubwise* (2010). He has published two books of short stories, *Uncle Obadiah and the Alien* (1997), and *Whose Your Daddy?* (2010); a novel, *Benjamin, My Son*, which was nominated for the IMPAC Dublin Literary Prize. He has also written two children's books, *Grandpa Sydney's Anancy Stories* and *Marcus and the Amazons*.

His poems and short stories are widely published, appearing in *Small Axe*, *Asili*, *The Caribbean Writer*, *Gulf Stream*, *Florida in Poetry: A History of the Imagination*, *Wheel and Come Again: An Anthology of Reggae Poetry*, *Whispers from the Cotton Tree Root*, *The Oxford Book of Caribbean Short Stories*, and *The Oxford Book of Caribbean Verse*.

He posts interviews, fiction, poetry, podcasts, and literary events from the Caribbean and South Florida on his blog http://geoffreyphilp.blogspot.com

ALSO AVAILABLE

hurricane center
ISBN: 9781900715232; pp. 67; pub., 1998; £7.99

El nino stirs clouds over the Pacific. Flashing TV screens urge a calm that no one believes. The police beat a slouched body, crumpled like a fist of kleenex. The news racks are crowded with stories of pestilence, war and rumours of war. The children, once sepia-faced cherubim, mutate to monsters that eat, eat, eat. You notice a change in your body's conversation with itself, and in the garden the fire ants burrow into the flesh of the fruit.

These poems stare into the dark heart of a world where hurricanes, both meteorological and metaphorical, threaten you to the last cell. But the sense of dread also reveals what is most precious in life, for the dark and accidental are put in the larger context of season and human renewal, and *hurricane center* returns always to the possibilities of redemption and joy.

In the voices of Jamaican prophets, Cuban exiles, exotic dancers, drunks, race-track punters, canecutters, rastamen, middle-class householders and screw-face ghetto sufferers, Geoffrey Philp writes poetry which is both intimately human and cosmic in scale. On the airwaves between Miami and Kingston, the rhythms of reggae and mambo dance through these poems.

xango music
ISBN 9781900715461; pp. 64; pub., 2001; price £7.99

In the Xango ceremony, the contraries of New World African experience find transcendence. From the established, bodily patterns of ritual comes release into the freedom of the spirit; from the exposure of pain comes the possibilities of healing; and for the individual there is both the dread aloneness with the gods and the 'we-ness' of community.

Simultaneously the rites celebrate the rich, syncretic diversity, the multiple connections of the African person in the New World and enact the tragic search for the wholeness of the lost African centre. And there is the god himself, standing at the crossroads, 'beating iron into the shape of thunder', both the prophetic voice warning of the fire to command the creator who hammers out sweet sound from the iron drum.

Geoffrey Philp finds in Xango a powerful metaphor that is both particular to the Caribbean and universal in its relevance. If his first collection, *Florida Bound*, was characterised by the exile's bittersweet elegies of regret, and the second, *hurricane center*, stared edgily into the dark heart of a threatening world, *xango music* brings a new sinewy toughness of line to an ever deepening vision of the dynamic polarities of human existence.

David and Phyllis Gershator writes in *The Caribbean Writer*: "Using rhythm and riffs, he can pull the stops on language and give it a high energy kick. In 'jam-rock'' he winds up with 'the crack of bones, the sweat of the whip; girl, you gonna get a lot of it; get it galore; my heart still beats uncha, uncha uncha, cha'.

Philp successfully uses a variety of traditional forms, including the sestina – not an easy form to master but masterfully handled in "sestina for bob." Eclectic, the poet pays homage to Kamau Brathwaite, Bob Marley, and Derek Walcott.

Dubwise
ISBN   9781845231712; pp. 72; pub., 2020;price £8.99

"Without losing the joy of play or the play of the rhythms, *Dub Wise* celebrates the burdens and delights of love, friendships and the responsibility of being at home in the world. Geoffrey Philp's new book is witty, playful, gracious and, yes, wise. An enjoyable read from beginning to end." – Olive Senior.

"The voice now distinctive, recognizable, the tone clear & clipped & 'skitter' [the 'something like music'], the stanzas running into each separate other, as they shd, like the human voice does. Also a new strong sense of place (Third World Miami and its Spanish – and Kgn of course – esp from Mountain View to the Sea), family & history (welcome the Seminole).

Above all, there is the continuing infolding of a 'Jamaica Tradition' as being established in the voices of Morris & Dawes, plus also the acknowledgment of McNeill, Baugh, Mikey Smith & Garvey, and the NL of Jean Binta Breeze. And Derek Walcott (where he grounds, in a way, the Morris-Dawes Ja Tradition) in 'Beyond Mountain View'".

— Kamau Brathwaite